BURKINA FASO

EXECUTIVE SUMMARY

Burkina Faso is a presidential republic. In November 2010 President Blaise Compaore was reelected to a fourth term with more than 80 percent of the vote. Despite some irregularities and the resource advantage held by the president, international observers considered the election to have been free and transparent. The president, assisted by members of his party, the Congress for Democracy and Progress (CDP), continued to dominate the government. The CDP won a majority in the 2007 legislative elections, which observers declared generally free and orderly despite irregularities, including fraud involving voter identification cards. There were instances in which elements of the security forces acted independently of civilian control.

Major human rights problems included security force use of excessive force against civilians, criminal suspects, and detainees; abuse of prisoners and harsh prison conditions; and societal violence and discrimination against women and children, including female genital mutilation.

Other major abuses included arbitrary arrest and detention, judicial inefficiency and lack of independence, official corruption, trafficking in persons, discrimination against persons with disabilities, and child labor.

The government took steps to prosecute individuals in the police and military accused of human rights abuse. However, impunity remained a problem in the country.

Section 1. Respect for the Integrity of the Person, Including Freedom from:

a. Arbitrary or Unlawful Deprivation of Life

The government or its agents did not commit any politically motivated killings. However, on February 20, Justin Zongo, a 24-year old high school student, died in a Koudougou hospital. Zongo was questioned by police several times between December 2010 and February 2011 after a female classmate pressed charges against him for battery. Students and civil society organizations claimed that Zongo died as a result of police brutality, and not of meningitis as the government initially claimed. This death sparked violent protests first in the Koudougou area and then throughout the country. In the days following Zongo's death, the confrontations between protesters and security forces turned violent. A total of five civilians were killed in separate incidents by stray bullets when the overwhelmed police tried to keep the crowd under control and protect government buildings. On February 23, students Wendkuni Kissou and Assad Ouedraogo and mechanic Issa Bado died after clashes with security forces in Koudougou. Students Ahmed Zougba in Poa and Michel Bouda in Kindi died on February 24. Policeman Andre Dabire was lynched by a mob in Poa the same day in retaliation for the deaths of civilians. According to the Burkina Faso Movement for Human and Peoples' Rights (MBDHP), live fire used by police and gendarmerie units during crowd control caused those deaths.

On February 26, the government responded to the violent protests by relieving the governor of the Central West region and the regional police director of their duties. On March 11, the Ministry of Justice indicted three policemen in connection with Justin Zongo's death and kept them in detention while investigations were underway. The attorney general later stated that the Ouagadougou Court of Appeal would investigate Zongo's death, and the incidents in Poa, Kindi, and Koudougou as separate events.

On August 23, the Ouagadougou Court of Appeal jury found two of the indicted policemen guilty of manslaughter and one of being an accessory to manslaughter in the death of Justin Zongo. They were sentenced respectively to 10 and eight years of imprisonment and immediately transferred to the city jail. The defendants' lawyers filed an appeal with the Cour de Cassation, the highest court of appeal in the country. The Criminal Chamber of the Cour de Cassation was called upon to try the three other cases. In the Koudougou incidents, two individuals were charged and were in jail pending trial at year's end. Regarding events in Poa, a policeman and two civilians were detained on murder, and destruction of public buildings and personal properties charges. In Kindi, a police assistant was arrested. At year's end investigations were underway with the judges ordering ballistic expertise in Koudougou and Kindi, and autopsies of the victims in the all cases.

In June 2010 Da Arnaud Some died while in police custody several hours after having been arrested in Danyoro for alleged drug possession. The circumstances of Some's death in a Gaoua hospital were unclear. According to the police, Some tried to escape and sustained injuries falling down a steep ravine. He died a few hours later in the hospital. Human rights organizations, including the MBDHP, investigated the death and concluded that Some died as a result of a police beating and not because of an alleged fall. The MBDHP called for an independent investigation and the arrest of those responsible for Some's death. The government took rapid disciplinary action, arresting the three policemen allegedly involved in Some's death and reassigning the entire police staffs in Danyoro and Gaoua, including the two chiefs of police, to other police stations. The three policemen were tried by the criminal chamber of the Bobo-Dioulasso Court of Appeal. On June 17, two of them were convicted of manslaughter and sentenced to five years in jail; charges were dropped against the third.

In July 2010 security forces killed two young men in Gaoua after violent demonstrations organized to protest the June 30 killing of Some. According to official reports, security forces used shotguns to restore order. Human rights associations collected empty cartridges after the incidents and said injuries were consistent with the use of live fire. Official post-incident reports referred to the causes of death as "accidental" (see section 1c).

b. Disappearance

There were no reports of politically motivated disappearances.

c. Torture and Other Cruel, Inhuman, or Degrading Treatment or Punishment

Although the constitution and law prohibit such treatment, members of the security forces continued to abuse individuals. The government made efforts to investigate and bring such cases to justice (see section 1.a). Suspects in police or gendarmerie custody reportedly were subjected frequently to beatings and threats. Government actions to prevent such treatment were limited, with only a few known cases when this behavior was punished. For example, in February four soldiers publically humiliated a civilian by forcing him to undress and parade naked (see section 1.d.).

Prison and Detention Center Conditions

Prisons and detention facilities did not meet international standards. Conditions in prisons and detention facilities were harsh and at times life-threatening. Prisons were overcrowded, and medical care and sanitation were poor. Although regulations require the presence of a doctor and five nurses at the Maison d'Arret et de Correction de Ouagadougou's (MACO) health unit, only three nurses are on duty to treat the 1,506 detainees. Prisoners' diets were inadequate, and inmates often relied on supplemental food from relatives. Typically, a designated group of detainees are tasked with cooking meals each day. Pretrial detainees usually were held with convicted prisoners. The infrastructures are decrepit and not adequately maintained. In some prisons such as the MACO, the severe overcrowding hinders appropriate ventilation. However, each cell has electricity and inmates can opt to buy a fan. They have access to potable water and rudimentary sanitation. There is not an office of the ombudsmen; however, the Burkina Faso Movement for the Emergence of Justice (MBEJUS) reported that it occasionally acted as ombudsman at the MACO. Women are held in a separate area of the prison, and their detention conditions are better than those of men, in large part because they are so few and thus have access to larger living spaces. According to human rights organizations, deaths from prison conditions or neglect occurred. Human rights activists believed that two to four inmates die every week as a result of prison conditions. In order to address overcrowding, the Ministry of Justice regularly grants provisional release to inmates who have served at least two-thirds of their sentences. Other alternative measures include community service and half way house.

According to the Ministry of Justice, as of December 17, there were 4,837 persons incarcerated countrywide, including 103 women and 102 minors. Juveniles and adults were not held together in Ouagadougou; however, in provincial prisons they were held together because no separate facilities existed for juveniles. Under the supervision of the Ministry of Justice, the Centre Laye houses convicted juveniles and provides them with training to help them transition back to jobs.

Prisoners and detainees had reasonable access to visitors and were permitted religious observance. Authorities permitted prisoners and detainees to submit complaints to judicial authorities without censorship and to request investigation of credible allegations of inhumane incarceration conditions. The government investigated and monitored prison and detention center conditions. Prison authorities granted permission to visit prisons without requiring advance notice for representatives of local and international human rights groups, the media, foreign embassies, and the International Committee of the Red Cross (ICRC). The ICRC visited prisons as did members of local nongovernmental organizations (NGOs), foreign embassies, and the press. The government conducted human rights and civil liberties training for security forces, including prison officers.

Two riots occurred in Ouagadougou and Bobo-Dioulasso prisons during the year. In Ouagadougou, on February16, a group of prisoners tried to escape from the MACO during the night. The attempt to tunnel out failed but turned into a riot after prison officers intervened. Prisoners demanded speedy trials, better diet and health care, and measures to alleviate overcrowding. An inmate was injured and a building was damaged due to a fire. After the incident, the minister of justice and human rights promotion visited the MACO and met with prisoners to discuss their demands. The MBEJUS reported that improvements were made, including efforts by the government to increase food rations and establish a better medication supply for the prison health unit.

Similar events took place in the Bobo-Dioulasso prison on April 1. After a failed escape attempt, a group of prisoners fought with prison guards. One prisoner was killed during the riot, and 10 others were injured.

The government conducted investigations on both prison incidents. As a result, 10 MACO inmates were charged with malicious damage of property, attempting to escape, and rebellion. They were sentenced to an additional 12 months in jail. Investigations were underway at year's end for Bobo-Dioulasso's prison.

d. Arbitrary Arrest or Detention

The constitution and law prohibit arbitrary arrest and detention; however, security forces did not consistently observe these prohibitions. The government did not take steps to prevent such treatment and did not systematically investigate and punish those responsible.

Role of the Police and Security Apparatus

The National Police, under the Ministry of Security, and the municipal police, under the Ministry of Territorial Administration, are responsible for public security. Gendarmes, under the Ministry of Security, are responsible for restoring law and order during a disturbance, enforcing the penal code, and taking preventive action, such as checking if individuals are carrying required official documents.

Human rights organizations stated that, although overall there was a climate of impunity, the government took steps to address police abuse. Policemen were convicted and sentenced to jail time in the Justin Zongo and Da Arnaud Some cases (see section 1 a). Security forces, particularly the army, sometimes acted independently of civilian control as illustrated by this year's multiple military mutinies.

On March 22, in response to actions after an altercation between a senior enlisted soldier and four of his soldier friends, on one side, and his wife's suspected lover, a Ouagadougou High Court sentenced four soldiers to 12 months in jail, and a fifth to 15 months and also a three million CFA fine (approximately $6,016) to cover damages to the victim. The judge found them guilty of public indecency and theft because they publicly had humiliated the wife's alleged lover in February by forcing him to undress and parade naked.

This court decision angered some of their fellow soldiers, who felt the sentences were too harsh. They decided to forcibly free their colleagues using their military-issued weapons, caused damaged to the courthouse, and succeeded in freeing their fellow soldiers from the base prison. The government, to avoid the escalation of violence, did not immediately re-incarcerate them. In protest, on March 24, magistrate and lawyers' unions announced a nationwide suspension of all judicial activities until the convicted soldiers were returned to prison. The soldiers were re-incarcerated on April 6 and are still awaiting trial; magistrates resumed their functions on April 11.

The criminal court of the Court of Appeals, however, granted the convicted soldiers provisional release on April 8, pending their appeal trial. The appeal trial was scheduled to take place on October 28, but the court postponed the trial to March 9, 2012.

In June soldiers mutinied to obtain better working conditions, new uniforms, and increased benefits. On July 7, the government published a presidential decree dismissing 566 soldiers for taking part in the mutiny. On December 15, an additional 60 soldiers were dismissed. In both instances, the charges cited were "particularly egregious conduct contrary to honor and morals, and incitement to public disorder." Among those dismissed in July, more than 308 were detained in military and civil jails and awaiting trial at year's end.

Observers stated that security forces were not effective in responding to societal violence. They pointed to complicated procedures for authorizing security force action as a hindrance to preventing and responding to societal violence. For example, authorities were not effective in addressing incidents last year between Fulani herders and Mossi, Gourounsi, and Gourmanche farmers, or in cases in which elderly women accused of witchcraft, were expelled from their homes or villages.

The Justice and Human Rights Promotion Ministry conducted seminars during the year to educate security forces on human rights.

Arrest Procedures and Treatment While in Detention

By law, police must possess a warrant based on sufficient evidence issued by authorized officials to apprehend a suspect; however, in practice these rights were not always respected. Detainees were not consistently informed of charges against them. The law provides the right to expeditious arraignment, bail, access to legal counsel after a detainee has been charged before a judge or, if indigent, access to a lawyer provided by the state after being charged; however, these rights were seldom respected. The law does not provide for detainees to have access to family members, although detainees generally were allowed such access through court-issued authorizations.

Arbitrary Arrest: The law limits detention without charge for investigative purposes to a maximum of 72 hours, renewable for a single 48-hour period; however, police rarely observed the law. The law permits judges to impose an unlimited number of six-month preventive detention periods. The average time of detention without charge (preventive detention) was one week. Defendants without access to legal counsel often were detained for weeks or months before appearing before a magistrate. For nonviolent offenders, ombudsmen are permitted to serve on behalf of prisoners and detainees to negotiate alternatives to incarceration to alleviate inhumane overcrowding.

Pretrial Detention: Government officials estimated that 48 percent of prisoners nationwide were in pretrial status. In some cases detainees were held without charge or trial for longer periods than the maximum sentence they would have received if convicted of the alleged offense. A pretrial release (release on bail) system exists; however, the extent of its use was unknown. Human rights advocates stated that the justice system, including prisons, had unreliable mechanisms to track detainees and occasionally "lost" some of them and/or their paperwork.

e. Denial of Fair Public Trial

The constitution and law provide for an independent judiciary; however, NGOs reported that the judiciary was corrupt, inefficient, and subject to executive influence. Constitutionally, the head of state also serves as president of the Superior Council of the Magistrature, which nominates and removes senior magistrates and examines their performance. Other systemic weaknesses in the justice system included corruption of magistrates, outdated legal codes, insufficient number of courts, and excessive legal costs.

Military courts try cases only involving military personnel charged with violation of the military code of conduct while on duty, and provide rights equivalent to those in civil criminal courts. Military courts are headed by a civilian judge. They hold public trials and publish verdicts in the local press.

Trial Procedures

Trials are public, but juries are only used for criminal cases. Defendants are presumed innocent and have the right to legal representation and consultation. Defendants have the right to be present at their trials, to be informed promptly of charges against them, to provide their own evidence, and to have access to government-held evidence. Defendants can challenge and present witnesses and have the right of appeal. In civil cases where the defendant is destitute and makes the request, the state provides a court-appointed lawyer. In criminal cases, court-appointed lawyers are mandatory for those who cannot afford it. However, these rights were not always respected, due in part to popular ignorance of the law and a continuing shortage of magistrates and court-appointed lawyers. Human rights organizations claim that there were major court backlogs but according to the Ministry of Justice and Human Rights Promotion, 74.8 percent of cases are tried within three months of formal indictment.

Political Prisoners and Detainees

There were no reports of political prisoners or detainees.

Civil Judicial Procedures and Remedies

There is an independent judiciary in civil matters; however, due to the corruption, lack of trust, and inefficiency of the judiciary, citizens sometimes preferred to rely on the ombudsman (see section 5) to settle disputes with the government. The law provides for access to a court to bring lawsuits seeking damages for, or cessation of, a human rights violation, and both administrative and judicial remedies were available for alleged wrongs. Several such court orders were issued during the year. There were problems enforcing court orders in sensitive cases involving national security, wealthy or influential persons, and government officials.

Property Restitution

The constitution provides women with equal property and inheritance rights. In practice, however, the courts did not consistently uphold a woman's right to inheritance. This practice was most prevalent in rural areas, where a widow's right of inheritance was superseded by her deceased husband's family claim on land and possessions.

f. Arbitrary Interference with Privacy, Family, Home, or Correspondence

The constitution and law prohibit such actions, and the government generally respects these prohibitions in practice. These rights were suspended in cases of national security, where the law permits surveillance, searches, and monitoring of telephones and private correspondence without a warrant.

Section 2. Respect for Civil Liberties, Including:

a. Freedom of Speech and Press

Status of Freedom of Speech and Press

The constitution and law provide for freedom of speech and of the press, and the government generally respected these rights in practice. Government media outlets including newspaper, television, and radio displayed a progovernment bias, but allowed significant participation in their newspaper and television programming by those representing opposition views. There were numerous independent newspapers, satirical weeklies, and radio and television stations, some of which were highly critical of the government. Foreign radio stations broadcast without government interference.

Individuals could criticize the government publicly or privately without reprisal. During the year the government did not attempt to impede criticism. All media are under the administrative and technical supervision of the Ministry of Communications, which is responsible for developing and implementing government policy and projects concerning information and communication. The Superior Council of Communication (SCC), a semiautonomous body under the Office of the President, also regulates the media by overseeing the content of radio and television programs and newspapers to ensure they adhere to professional ethics standards and government policy on information and communication. The SCC may summon a journalist to attend a hearing about his work, followed by a warning for any subsequent violations. Hearings may concern alleged libel, disturbing the peace, inciting violence, or violations of state security. After the death of Justin Zongo, the SCC repeatedly called for journalists and private newspapers to refrain from incendiary language and instead promote social peace. Some journalists saw this as a limitation of their freedom of speech.

Internet Freedom

There were no government restrictions on access to the Internet or reports that the government monitored e-mail or Internet chat rooms. Individuals and groups could engage in the peaceful expression of views via the Internet, including by e-mail.

Academic Freedom and Cultural Events

There were no government restrictions on academic freedom or cultural events.

b. Freedom of Peaceful Assembly and Association

Freedom of Assembly

The constitution and law provide for freedom of assembly; the government generally respected this right.

Political parties and labor unions may hold meetings and rallies without government permission; however, advance notification is required for demonstrations on the streets that might impact traffic or threaten public order. If a demonstration or rally results in violence, injuries, or significant property damage, penalties for the organizers include six months to five years of imprisonment, and fines comprised between 100,000 and 2 million CFA ($200 and $4,000). These penalties may be doubled for an unauthorized rally or demonstration. Denials or imposed modifications of a proposed march route or schedule may be appealed to the courts. Government agents sometimes infiltrated political meetings and rallies.

The government at times reportedly limited communications by disabling text message service on telephone networks. Human rights groups alleged that during the March and April student protests, the government employed such tactics.

On February 23 and 24, demonstrations in Koudougou, Poa, and Kindi following Justin Zongo's death resulted in six deaths. According to the MBDHP and other observers, police units used teargas and live fire to disperse protesters (see section 1.a.).

Freedom of Association

The constitution and law provide for freedom of association, and the government generally respected this right. Political parties and labor unions could organize without government permission.

c. Freedom of Religion

See the Department of State's *International Religious Freedom Report* at www.state.gov/j/drl/irf/rpt.

d. Freedom of Movement, Internally Displaced Persons, Protection of Refugees, and Stateless Persons

The constitution provides for freedom of movement within the country, foreign travel, emigration, and repatriation, and the government generally respected these rights in practice. The government cooperated with the Office of the UN High Commissioner for Refugees (UNHCR) and other humanitarian organizations to provide protection and assistance to internally displaced persons, refugees, returning refugees, asylum seekers, stateless persons, and other persons of concern.

The government, in accordance with the Economic Community of West African States' guidelines, required travel documents, such as identification cards, for regional travel.

Protection of Refugees

Access to Asylum: The country's laws provide for the granting of asylum or refugee status, and the government has established a system for providing protection to refugees. The government granted refugee or asylum status and also provided temporary protection to individuals who may not qualify as refugees under the 1951 Refugee Convention or its 1967 Protocol.

Access to Basic Services: Under the law, refugees have equal access to employment, basic services, education, police, and court services. There were no reports of refugees being denied these rights during the year.

Temporary Protection: According to the UNHCR and the National Commission for Refugees, 78 Ivoirian asylum-seekers were registered in Burkina Faso in April due to the Ivoirian political crisis. The majority resided in Ouagadougou.

Section 3. Respect for Political Rights: The Right of Citizens to Change Their Government

The constitution provides citizens with the right to change their government peacefully through multiparty elections; however, the ruling party's control of official resources and dominance in the government severely disadvantaged the political opposition.

Elections and Political Participation

Recent Elections: In November 2010 President Blaise Compaore won reelection with more than 80 percent of the vote. Opposition candidate Hama Arba Diallo, the runner-up, received 7.96 percent. Despite some irregularities, international observers considered the election to have been free and transparent despite the resource advantage held by the president.

Political Parties: Political parties operated freely. Individuals and parties may declare their candidacies and stand for election in presidential elections provided the Constitutional Council validates their candidacy; however, individuals must be members of a registered political party to run in legislative or municipal elections.

In the 2007 legislative elections, the ruling CDP won 73 seats in the 111-seat National Assembly. Of the 38 non-CDP members of parliament, 25 belonged to parties allied with the government. Election observers declared the elections free and orderly, except in four cities where they noted irregularities, including several cases of fraud involving voter identification cards. Opposition leaders denounced the elections.

CDP membership conferred advantages, particularly for businessmen and traders seeking ostensibly open government contracts.

There were no cabinet members from the political opposition

Participation of Women and Minorities: There were 16 women in the 111-seats National Assembly and three women in the 30-member presidential cabinet. One of the four higher courts was led by a woman, the national ombudsman was a woman, 22 elected mayors were women, and an estimated 40 to 45 percent of new communal councilors were women. There are more than 60 ethnic groups in the country. Major ethnic groups include Mossi (50 percent of the population),

Fulanis (12 percent), and Dioula (10 percent). Ethnicity is not a factor in cabinet appointments.

Section 4. Official Corruption and Government Transparency

The law provides criminal penalties for official corruption; however, the government did not enforce the law effectively, and officials often engaged in corrupt practices with impunity. Local NGOs denounced what they called the overwhelming corruption of senior civil servants. They reported that corruption was especially acute in the customs service, gendarmerie, taxing agencies, national police, municipal police, public health service, municipalities, the education sector, government procurement, and the Ministry of Justice and Human Right Promotion. In recent years, despite numerous alleged instances of high-level corruption, no senior government officials were prosecuted for corruption. On July 27, the Council of Ministers dismissed the mayors of Nangreongo and Boulmiougou because of accusations of embezzlement and mishandling of communal resources. At year's end the Ministry of Justice and Human Rights Promotion indicated that the High Courts of Ouagadougou and Ziniare have not prosecuted these cases.

Corruption was widespread, particularly among lower levels of police and gendarmerie. The 2010 report by the National Network to Fight Against Corruption, a nongovernmental organization, stated that customs, police, the health sector and tax offices were among the most corrupt institutions in the country. Corruption and official impunity were also a problem in the military. The gendarmerie is responsible for investigating abuse by police and gendarmes, but the results of their investigations were not always made public. The military courts held a number of trials in which civilians pressed charges against military personnel. These trials were public, and verdicts were reported in the press. The government took some judicial action against representatives of security forces accused by human rights groups of being responsible for abuses and took disciplinary action against policemen (see section 1.a.) and soldiers accused of looting and mutiny. At year's end 308 soldiers were detained for their role in the mutinies and are awaiting trial. On July 7, 566 were dismissed from their position by presidential decree as were another 60 on December 15.

Some public officials like the president, the prime minister, cabinet members, heads of institutions, ambassadors, and directors of state-owned companies are subject to financial disclosure laws, but anticorruption NGOs complain that those disclosures are not made public.

No laws provide for public access to government information. While government ministries released some nonsensitive documents, local journalists complained that ministries generally were unresponsive to requests for information, ostensibly for reasons of national security and confidentiality. There is no procedure to appeal denials of requests for information.

On July 20, the Council of Ministers adopted a new government communication strategy to improve accountability and transparency. The new measures, already in effect, include: a toll-free number for citizens seeking information on governmental action; a weekly column in newspapers; press conferences every Thursday; and production of television and radio shows. In 2009 and in an effort to fight corruption, the government also implemented a toll-free number to allow citizens to report suspected cases of corruption involving civil servants.

Section 5. Governmental Attitude Regarding International and Nongovernmental Investigation of Alleged Violations of Human Rights

A variety of domestic and international human rights groups operated without government restriction, investigating and publishing their findings on human rights cases. Government officials were cooperative and responsive to their views.

The government permitted international human rights groups to visit and operate in the country; the International Red Cross visited during the year.

The Ministry of Justice and Human Rights Promotion is responsible for the protection and promotion of human rights and coordinates relevant efforts of other ministries. The minister of justice and human rights promotion reports to the prime minister. During the year the ministry conducted education campaigns and published pamphlets to raise awareness of human rights among security force members.

Government Human Rights Bodies: The ombudsman is appointed by the president for a nonrenewable five-year term and cannot be removed during the term. The public generally trusted the ombudsman's impartiality. In accordance with the law, the ombudsman presented his 2010 report to the president on June 9. The institution investigates complaints related to conflicts between Burkinabe and non-Burkinabe nationals living in Burkina Faso and complaints involving government services. In 2010 the institution investigated 528 of the 880 registered complaints. The ombudsman office pursued 145 cases but was unsuccessful in negotiating a settlement in 30 cases.

The governmental National Commission on Human Rights serves as a permanent framework for dialogue on human rights concerns and included representatives of human rights NGOs, unions, professional associations, and the government. The MBDHP did not participate in the commission and continued to charge that the commission was subject to government influence. According to NGOs, the commission was inadequately funded and thus ineffective.

Section 6. Discrimination, Societal Abuses, and Trafficking in Persons

The constitution and law prohibit discrimination based on race, gender, disability, language, or social status; however, the government did not effectively enforce these prohibitions. Discrimination against women and persons with disabilities remained problems.

Women

Rape and Domestic Violence: Rape is a crime. Although there were prosecutions during the year, no official statistics were available on the number of rapes reported. Article 417 of the Penal Code makes rape punishable with five to 10 years' imprisonment. Human rights associations reported rape occurs frequently. The law makes no explicit mention of spousal rape, and there have been no recent court cases. Several organizations counseled rape victims, including Roman Catholic and Protestant missions, the Association of Women Jurists in Burkina, the MBDHP, the Association of Women, and Promofemmes (a regional network that works to combat violence against women). Once a rape is reported, police investigate the accusation and, if the evidence warrants, bring the case to court.

Domestic violence against women occurred frequently, primarily in rural areas. No law specifically protects women from domestic violence, and cases of wife beating usually were handled out of court. There were no available statistics on how many persons were prosecuted, convicted, or punished for domestic violence during the year. Such legal actions were infrequent, because women were ashamed, afraid, or otherwise reluctant to take their spouses to court. Cases that involve severe injury were usually handled through the legal system. There are no government-run shelters in the country for women victims of domestic violence, but there are counseling centers in each of the 13 regional "Maison de la Femme" structures. In addition, a toll-free help number was activated. Since December, there have been daily advertisements publishing the number in local papers.

The Ministry for Promotion of Women, the Ministry for Social Action and National Solidarity, and several NGOs cooperated to protect women's rights. The legal section in the Ministry for the Promotion of Women has a legal affairs section that informs women of their rights and encourages them to defend those rights. It organized a number of workshops and led several sensitization campaigns to inform women of their rights. Although the fight to achieve effective rights for women is a longstanding process, increasing numbers of women, primarily in urban areas, voiced their demand for equal rights. The numbers of women occupying decision-making positions has increased, with many active in politics. The government enacted a gender quota law in April 2009. This law requires that political parties have at least 30 percent women among candidates on their electoral lists for legislative and municipal elections. The law is scheduled to take effect during the 2012 elections and establishes financial incentives for political parties who reach the 30 percent threshold.

In July 2009 the government adopted a national gender policy aimed at reducing inequalities and gender discrimination in the country. At years' end the Ministry for Promotion of Women launched a national sensitization campaign focused on abating early and forced marriage and teen pregnancies.

On occasion, vulnerable elderly women with no support, primarily in rural areas and often widowed, were accused of witchcraft by fellow villagers and banned from their villages. They are often accused of eating the soul of a relative or a child who had died. These women sought refuge at centers run by governmental or charitable organizations in urban centers.

The Ministry of Social Action and National Solidarity recorded nearly 500 such women accused of being witches who had fled their villages. During the year the Roman Catholic-operated Delwende center housed approximately 317 persons accused of witchcraft. The Ministry of Social Action and National Solidarity provides financial assistance to the Delwende center and is building another center nearby to relocate them in an area not prone to flooding. Another similar government-run center is located in the Paspanga area in Ouagadougou and houses approximately 100 women. The government and traditional authorities worked together during the year to stop such persecutions. In particular, the Ministry of Social Action and National Solidarity initiated specific awareness programs with ethnic Mossi villages and assisted with mediation efforts between suspected "witches" and village elders. As part of an NGO-led sensitization campaign, women from the two centers demonstrated peacefully on March 6 in Ouagadougou. The Mogho Naaba, Emperor of the Mossi, was the sponsor of this event and wrote a letter denouncing the condition of these women and calling for an end to this practice.

Sexual Harassment: The labor code explicitly prohibits sexual harassment in the workplace, but such harassment of women was common and considered by many as culturally acceptable. The law prescribes fines of 50,000 to 600,000 CFA francs ($100 to $1,203) and prison terms varying from one month to five years for persons convicted of workplace harassment. There were no available statistics on how many persons were prosecuted, convicted, or punished for the offense during the year.

Reproductive Rights: Couples and individuals are legally entitled to decide freely and responsibly the number, spacing, and timing of their children. They have the right to access reproductive and family planning information and may do so without facing discrimination, coercion, or violence. In practice, however, a lack of access to information and medical care constrained these rights, especially in remote areas. Cultural norms, especially in rural areas with less educated populations, also limited the availability and use of these resources. Reproductive rights were usually respected in urban areas and among more educated people. According to the 2010 demographic and health survey preliminary report (published in August 2011), the modern contraceptive prevalence rate is 15 percent. A DHS preliminary report also shows that 67 percent of births were attended by skilled personnel. However, women often were subject to their husbands' decision regarding birth control. In 2008 UNICEF estimated that the maternal mortality ratio was 560 deaths per 100,000 live births, that a woman's lifetime risk of maternal death was one in 28, and that a total of 54 percent of births were attended by skilled personnel (mainly midwives).

Both government and private health centers were open to all women for reproductive health services, including contraception, skilled medical assistance during childbirth (essential obstetric and postpartum care), and diagnosis and treatment of sexually transmitted diseases. However, remote villages often lacked these facilities or did not have adequate road infrastructure and transportation to permit easy access. To obtain specific treatment or deliver under medical supervision, women in rural areas sometimes had to travel great distances to the closest urban health center. According to Amnesty International, maternal deaths could also be partly explained by health workers lacking adequate training.

Discrimination: Women continued to occupy a subordinate position in society and often experienced discrimination in education, jobs, property ownership, access to credit, management or ownership of a business, and family rights. Polygyny is permitted, but both parties have to agree to it prior to marriage. A wife may oppose further marriages by her husband if she provides evidence that he has abandoned her and her children. Each spouse may petition for divorce, and the law provides that custody of a child may be granted to either parent, based on the child's best interest. In practice, however, the mother retained custody until the child reached the age of seven, at which time custody reverted to the father or his family. Women represented approximately 45 percent of the general workforce in the formal sector and were primarily concentrated in lower-paying subservient positions. Although the law provides equal property rights for women and, depending on other family relationships, inheritance benefits, traditional law often denied women the right to own property, particularly real estate. This is exacerbated by the fact that 75 percent of marriages are defined as common law (religious or traditional ceremony) marriages and not legally binding. For example, in rural areas, land owned by a woman becomes the property of the family of her husband after marriage. Many citizens, particularly in rural areas, clung to traditional beliefs that did not recognize inheritance rights for women and regarded a woman as property that could be inherited upon her husband's death.

The government continued media campaigns to change attitudes toward women, but progress was slow. The Ministry for Women's Promotion is responsible for increasing women's awareness of their rights, and is working to facilitate their access to land. The government sponsored a number of community outreach efforts and awareness campaigns to promote women's rights.

Children

Birth Registration: Citizenship is derived either by birth within the country's territory or through a parent. Many births are not registered immediately, particularly in rural areas where administrative structures are insufficient, geographically distant, and rural parents do not know such registration is required. Lack of registration sometimes resulted in denial of public services and inability to register for school. To address the problem, the government periodically organized registration drives and issued belated birth certificates.

Education: The law calls for compulsory, tuition-free, and universal education until the age of 16. The government paid tuition, books, and supplies for all students under 16 years of age, although uniforms were the responsibility of the student's family. Children over 16 years of age were responsible for paying all education costs, unless they qualified for tuition assistance from merit-and need-based programs. The overall primary, school enrollment was approximately 78 percent for boys and 71 percent for girls.

Child Abuse: The law prohibits the abuse of children under 15 and provides for the punishment of abusers. The penal code mandates a one-to three-year prison sentence and fines ranging from 300,000 to 900,000 CFA francs ($601 to $1,805) for inhumane treatment or mistreatment of children; however, light corporal punishment was tolerated and widely practiced in society, although the government conducted seminars and education campaigns against child abuse.

In September, 29 year-old Boukary Sawadogo was convicted and sentenced to three years in jail for public indecency and sexually abusing a minor.

On September 13, the Ministry of Social Action and National Solidarity launched a toll-free number enabling people to anonymously report cases of violence against children. During the year the ministry equipped two care centers in Ouagadougou and Bobo-Dioulasso for child victims.

Child Marriage: Several NGOs stated that child marriage was a problem. In rural areas, the Population Council estimated that, in 2009, 62 percent of girls and women aged between 20 and 24 were married by the age of 18. In the Sahel region, 19 percent of girls are married before 15. According to the law, the legal age for marriage is 17 for women and 20 for men. The law prohibits forced marriage and prescribes penalties of six months to two years in prison for violation. The prison term may be increased to three years, if the victim is less than 13 years of age; however, there were no reports during the year of prosecutions of violators. Many NGOs worked with traditional leaders and village elders to halt this practice. From 2008 to 2010, the government carried out a project called "Getting rid of early marriages in Burkina Faso: a plan for protection, accountability and community's intervention." The project aimed at fighting early marriage by strengthening young girls' skills and their civil rights knowledge.

Harmful Traditional Practices: Female genital mutilation (FGM) was practiced, especially in rural areas, despite being illegal, and usually was performed at an early age. Although there are no accurate and recent figures on FGM, the National Committee for the Fight Against Excision (CNLPE) believes that the practice has decreased significantly in recent years. In 2008 the committee reported that 249 girls had undergone FGM, but this number should take into consideration the fact that some parents take their child to neighboring countries, such as Mali, where the practice of FGM is legal. Perpetrators are subject to a significant fine of 150,000 to 900,000 CFA (between $301 and $1,811), and imprisonment of six months to three years, or up to 10 years if the victim dies. During the year security forces and social workers from the Ministry of Social Action and National Solidarity arrested several FGM practitioners and their accomplices. In accordance with the law, they were sentenced to prison terms. On September 16, the Bobo-Dioulasso High Court sentenced Daouda Konate to three years in jail and a fine for perpetrating FGM on four girls under the age of three. It was the first time that a man was convicted of FGM.

Burkina Faso's First Lady Chantal Compaore is the honorary president of the CNLPE and is actively involved in the fight against FGM. On February 28, she chaired a roundtable at the UN headquarters entitled: "International Campaign for a United Nations General Assembly Resolution to Ban FGM Worldwide".

The government, through the Regional Committees to Combat Excision, continued to work with local populations to address FGM. These regional committees (presided over by government-appointed high commissioners) brought together representatives of the Ministries of Social Action, Basic Education, Secondary and Superior Education, Women's Rights, Justice, Health, the police and gendarmerie, and local and religious leaders; they actively campaigned against the practice.

The government continued its national action plan, a "Zero Tolerance to FGM" that aimed to reduce the practice of FGM by at least 30 percent by year 2013. Towards that end during the year the government conducted awareness campaigns, trainings, and identification and support programs for victims of this practice. In September the Network of Burkina Faso Islamic Organizations organized a national conference to raise awareness and fight against FGM. They explained that despite popular belief, FGM is not a Muslim tradition.

Sexual Exploitation of Children: There were no statistics on child prostitution; however, government services and human rights associations believed it was a problem. Children from poor families relied on prostitution to meet their daily needs and, at times, to help their needy parents. Trafficked children, primarily Nigerian nationals, were also subject to sexual abuse and forced prostitution.

Infanticide: The law prohibits female infanticide, and there were no reports of such cases. Newspapers reported cases of abandonment of newborn babies following unwanted pregnancies.

Displaced Children: There were numerous street children, primarily in Ouagadougou and Bobo-Dioulasso. Many children ended up on the streets after traveling from rural areas to find employment in the city, after their parents sent them to the city to study with an unregistered Qur'an teacher, or to live with relatives and go to school. According to a 2010 report by the Ministry of Social Action and National Solidarity, there were 5,721 street children in Burkina Faso among which 2,308 children were enrolled in unregistered Qur'anic schools. Several NGOs assisted street children. Two directorates within the Ministry of Social Action and National Solidarity also ran educational programs, including vocational training, for street children; funded income-generating activities; and assisted in the reintegration and rehabilitation of street children. Nevertheless, the number of street children far outstripped the capacity of these institutions.

On September 10, the Regional Direction of Social Action and National Solidarity in the Cascades region (in the west) organized a workshop with members of the Muslim community, Qur'anic teachers, police, gendarmerie and social workers. They worked with and educated members of the Muslim community and discussed solutions to end the phenomenon of street children, particularly child-beggars in Qur'anic schools.

International Child Abductions: The country is a party to the 1980 Hague Convention on the Civil Aspects of International Child Abduction. For information see the Department of State's report on compliance at http://travel.state.gov/abduction/resources/congressreport/congressreport_4308.htm as well as country-specific information at http://travel.state.gov/abduction/country/country_3781.html.

Anti-Semitism

There were no reports of anti-Semitic acts. There was no known Jewish community in the country.

Trafficking in Persons

See the Department of State's *Trafficking in Persons Report* at www.state.gov/j/tip.

Persons with Disabilities

The law prohibits discrimination against persons with physical or mental disabilities in employment, education, access to health care, the provision of other state services, or other areas; however, the government did not effectively enforce these provisions. In April 2010 the government enacted additional legislation to expand the rights of persons with disabilities. The law provides for reduced-cost or free healthcare and access to education, and establishes codes for access to buildings, and access to employment persons with disabilities often faced societal and economic discrimination. Such persons who were able to work found it difficult to find employment, including in government service, because of deeply entrenched societal attitudes that persons with disabilities should be under the care of their families and not in the workforce.

Programs to aid persons with disabilities were limited. During the year the National Committee for the Reintegration of Persons with Disabilities and NGOs conducted awareness campaigns and implemented integration programs and capacity-building programs to manage income-generating activities better. High commissioners, teachers and NGOs worked together to inform citizens about the rights of persons with disabilities, specifically the rights of children with disabilities. A number of NGOs schooled and provided vocational training to persons with disabilities and provided equipment for them to work.

National/Racial/Ethnic Minorities

Incidents of conflict have flared over trampled fields involving cattle herders of the Fulani ethnic group and farmers of other ethnic groups. Such incidents were fueled by the scarcity of grazing lands and Fulani herders allowing their cattle to graze on farm lands of the other groups, or farmers wanting to cultivate land set aside by local authorities for grazing. According to the Ministry of Animal Resources, more than 3,800 of such conflicts occurred between 2005 and 2011, including 318 during the first half of 2011. These conflicts caused 55 deaths since 2005 (see section 1.d., Role of the Police and Security Apparatus).

In May clashes between members of Bwaba and Mossi ethnic groups occurred in Solenzo over alleged disrespect for a traditional Bwaba initiation ceremony by a Mossi. The confrontation resulted in two deaths. The governor of the region and local authorities went to Solenzo to mediate with local residents in order to resolve the conflict. This incident also reflected long-lasting tensions over land use in the region.

Societal Abuses, Discrimination, and Acts of Violence Based on Sexual Orientation and Gender Identity

The law does not discriminate on the basis of sexual orientation in employment and occupation, housing, statelessness, or access to education or health care. However, societal discrimination based on sexual orientation and gender identity remained a problem. Religious and traditional beliefs do not accept homosexuality, and lesbian, gay, bisexual, and transgender (LGBT) persons were reportedly occasional victims of verbal and physical abuse. There were no reports that the government responded to societal violence and discrimination against such persons.

LGBT organizations had no legal presence in the country but existed unofficially. There were no reports of government or societal violence against such organizations.

Other Societal Violence or Discrimination

Societal discrimination against persons with HIV/AIDS was a problem. During the year approximately 130,000 persons were HIV-positive, 1.8 percent of the population. Persons who tested positive were sometimes shunned by their families, and HIV-positive wives were sometimes evicted from their homes while their husbands were not. Some landlords refused to rent lodgings to persons with HIV/AIDS. However, persons with HIV/AIDS were generally not discriminated against in employment practices or the workplace. In January 2010 the government announced free distribution of antiretroviral medication for HIV-positive persons.

Section 7. Worker Rights

a. Freedom of Association and the Right to Collective Bargaining

The law allows workers to form and join independent unions of their choice without previous authorization or excessive requirements; however, "essential" workers such as police, army, and other security personnel may not join unions. The law provides unions the right to conduct their activities without interference.

The law provides for the right to strike, although it stipulates a very narrow definition of this right. For strikes that call on workers to stay home and that do not entail participation in a rally, the union is required to send an advance notice (eight to 15 days) to the government. If unions call for a march, then the government requires the same request and that a notice also be submitted to the concerned city mayor. March organizers are held accountable for any damage or property destruction that occurs during the demonstration. Magistrates, police, military personnel, and gendarmes do not have the right to strike.

The law prohibits anti-union discrimination and allows a labor inspector to immediately reinstate workers fired because of their union activities. All workers without distinction benefit from the relevant legal protections. The government generally enforced these laws.

The government respected freedom of association and the right to collective bargaining. During the year the government received 16 requests for union recognition. All were granted. The government respected the right to conduct their activities without interference.

Unions have the right to bargain directly with employers and industry associations for wages and other benefits. Approximately 86 percent of the work force was engaged in subsistence agriculture and did not belong to unions. Of the remainder, an estimated 25 percent of private sector employees and 60 percent of public sector workers were union members. Worker organizations are independent of the government and political parties. There were no reports of strikebreaking during the year.

There were no reports of government restrictions on collective bargaining during the year. There was extensive collective bargaining in the formal wage sector; however, this sector included only a small percentage of workers. Moreover, employers sometimes refused to bargain with unions. This was the case for the establishment of an inter-professional collective convention. In the private sector, particularly in the mining sector and other industries, employers' use of subcontracting made it difficult to systematically enforce workers rights.

There were no reports of antiunion discrimination during the year.

b. Prohibition of Forced or Compulsory Labor

The law prohibits forced or compulsory labor, including by children; however, there were reports that such practices occurred. Forced child labor was found in the country's agricultural (particularly cotton), informal trade, domestic servitude, and animal husbandry sectors as well as in gold panning sites and stone quarries.

Some children sent to Qur'anic schools by their parents were forced to engage in begging (see section 6, displaced children).

There were no instances of compulsory participation in public works or forced prison labor.

Also see the Department of State's *Trafficking in Persons Report* at www.state.gov/j/tip.

c. Prohibition of Child Labor and Minimum Age for Employment

The law sets the minimum age for employment at 16 and prohibits children less than 18 years of age from working at night except in times of emergency. The minimum age for employment was consistent with the age for completing educational requirements, which was 16 years. In the domestic and agricultural sectors, the law permits children under the age of 15 to perform limited activities for up to four and one-half hours per day. There were no explicit restrictions regarding occupational health and safety in the law.

The law prohibits the worst forms of child labor, including the commercial sexual exploitation of children, child pornography, and jobs that harm their health. The 2008 antitrafficking legislation provides for penalties of up to 10 years for violators and increases maximum prison terms from five to 10 years. The law also allows terms as high as 20 years to life imprisonment under certain conditions. However, the government did not effectively enforce the law.

The Ministry of Civil Service, Labor and Social Security, which oversees labor standards, lacked the financial and transportation means as well as a sufficient number of inspectors to enforce worker safety and minimum age legislation adequately. Punishment for violating child labor laws included prison terms of up to five years and fines of up to 600,000 CFA francs ($1,207). The number of convictions during the year was unknown.

The government organized workshops during the year, and in cooperation with donors, undertook sensitization programs to inform children, parents, and employers of the dangers of exploitative child labor and sending children away from home to work. The government worked with local NGOs to monitor the opening of new gold mines to ensure that no children were employed there illegally.

Child labor was a problem. According to the National Institute of Statistics and Demography 41.1 percent of the children between five and 17 years were engaged in some form of economic activity. Children mostly worked in the following areas: agriculture (69.2 percent), mining (2.2 percent), trade (5 percent) and sometimes as domestic servants in the informal sector (19 percent). Some children, particularly those working as cattle herders and street hawkers did not attend school. A 2010 UNICEF study found that of 50,000 gold miners, 19,881 were children. The main reason for this phenomenon was poverty and insufficient access to education.

Many children under the age of 15 worked long hours. Children commonly worked with their parents in rural areas or in family-owned small businesses in villages and cities. There were no reports of children under age 15 employed in either state-owned or large private companies.

Also see the Department of Labor's *Findings on the Worst Forms of Child Labor* at www.dol.gov/ilab/programs/ocft/tda.htm

d. Acceptable Conditions of Work

The law mandates a minimum monthly wage of 30,684 CFA francs ($61) in the formal sector; the minimum wage does not apply to subsistence agriculture or other informal occupations.

The law mandates a standard workweek of 40 hours for non-domestic workers and a 60-hour workweek for household employees, and it provides for overtime pay. There are also regulations pertaining to rest periods, limits on hours worked, and prohibition of excessive compulsory overtime, but these standards were not effectively enforced.

The government sets occupational health and safety standards. Every company with 10 or more employees is required to have a work safety committee. If the government's Labor Inspection Office declares a workplace unsafe for any reason, workers have the right to remove themselves without jeopardizing continued employment. The Ministry of Civil service, Labor and Social Security was responsible for enforcing the minimum wage. Government inspectors under the Ministry of Civil Service, Labor, and Social Security and the labor tribunals are responsible for overseeing occupational health and safety standards in the small industrial and commercial sectors, but these standards do not apply in subsistence agriculture and other informal sectors.

These standards were generally not effectively enforced. During the year the government in conjunction with the Action Catholique des Travailleurs provided technical assistance for trainings and seminars as well as workshops on legislation and workers rights. The government's Labor Inspector Corps did not have sufficient resources, including sufficient numbers of inspectors and offices and financial and transportation means, to fulfill its duties adequately. There were 125 labor inspectors and 116 labor controllers. There were no reports of effective enforcement of inspection findings during the year. There were indications that the right to remove oneself from unsafe working conditions was respected, although such declarations by the Labor Inspection Office were rare.

Employers often paid less than the minimum wage. Wage-earners usually supplemented their income through reliance on the extended family, subsistence agriculture, or trading in the informal sector.